Contents

1. Introduction
2. The rules
3. And we're off....
4. Let's double up....
5. Yellow car - Yellow car with black stripes on bonnet & black roof
6. Yellow car - Yellow car with white stripes on bonnet & white roof
7. Yellow car - Yellow soft top with white stripes on bonnet
8. Yellow car - Yellow soft top with black stripes on bonnet
9. Yellow car - Yellow car with white roof
10. Yellow car - Yellow car with black roof
11. Yellow car - Black car
12. Yellow car - Navy blue car
13. Yellow car - Light blue car
14. Yellow car - Gold Car
15. Yellow car - Green car
16. Yellow car - Red car
17. Yellow car - Pink car
18. Yellow car - Purple car
19. Yellow car - Brown car
20. Yellow car - Orange car
21. Yellow car - Grey car
22. Yellow car - Silver car
23. Yellow car - Bronze car
24. Yellow car - White car
25 - 27. Bonus pages

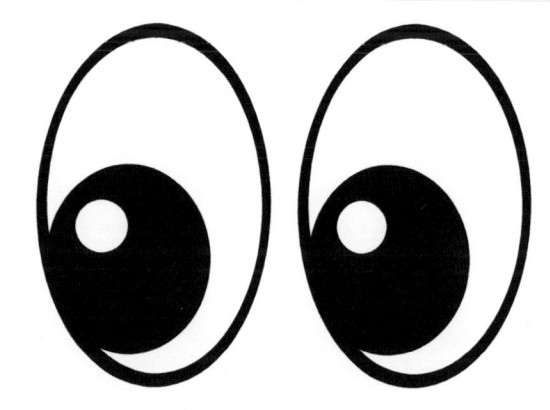

The Ultimate Yellow Car Spotters Handbook

Thank you for choosing the
Ultimate Yellow Car Spotters Book.

The aim of the game is to spot single yellow cars and double combinations using the 'tick' boxes to quickly record your 'spots'.

You can then colour the cars in later so you can keep a track of your progress.

Happy Yellow Car spotting!!!

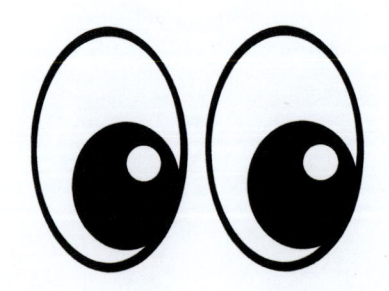

Simon Baldock

The rules....not that many :)

1. To count Yellow Cars must be moving and travelling on the opposite side of the road.

2. When spotting combinations, vehicles should not be more than two car lengths apart.

3. Have fun.....

Yellow Car 1

The Ultimate Yellow Car Spotters Handbook

And we're off

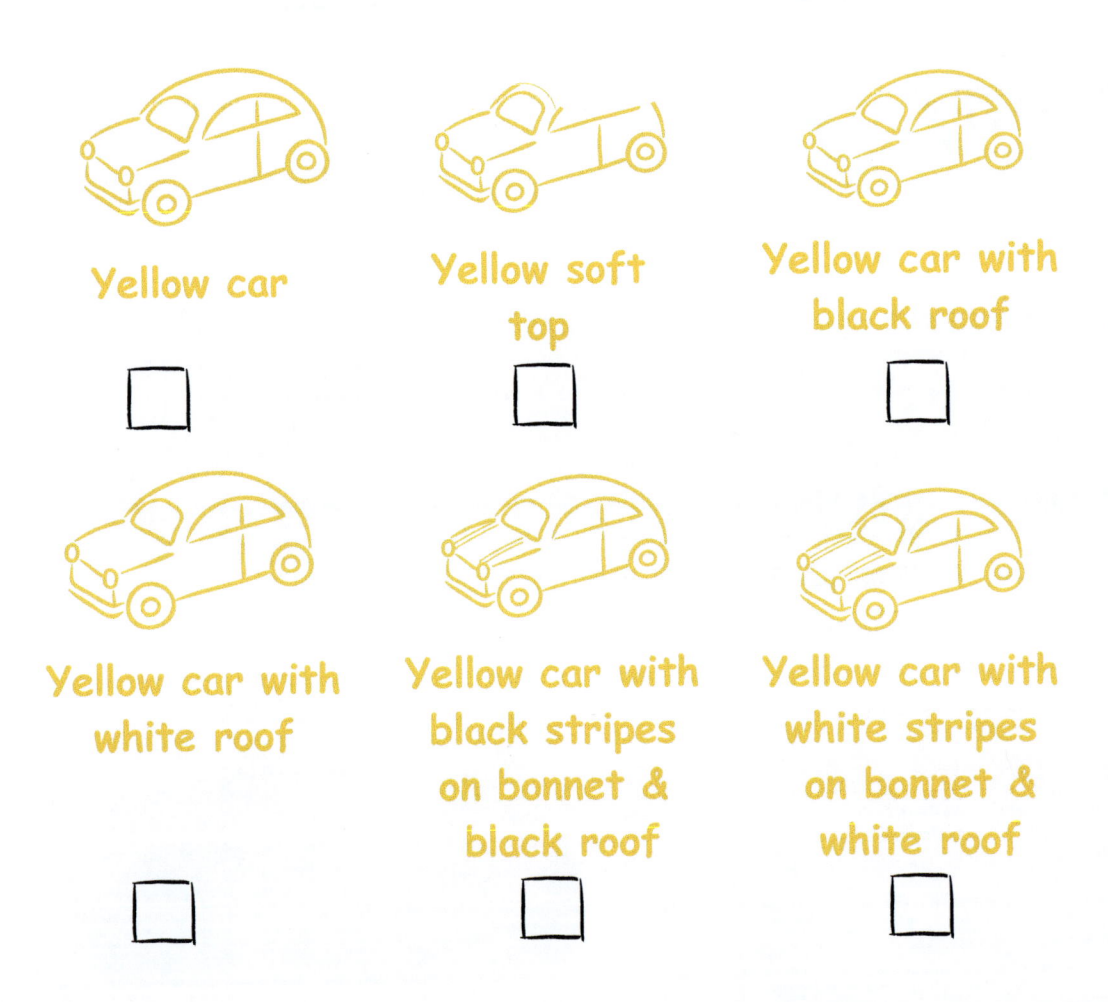

Yellow car ☐

Yellow soft top ☐

Yellow car with black roof ☐

Yellow car with white roof ☐

Yellow car with black stripes on bonnet & black roof ☐

Yellow car with white stripes on bonnet & white roof ☐

Lets double up!!!!

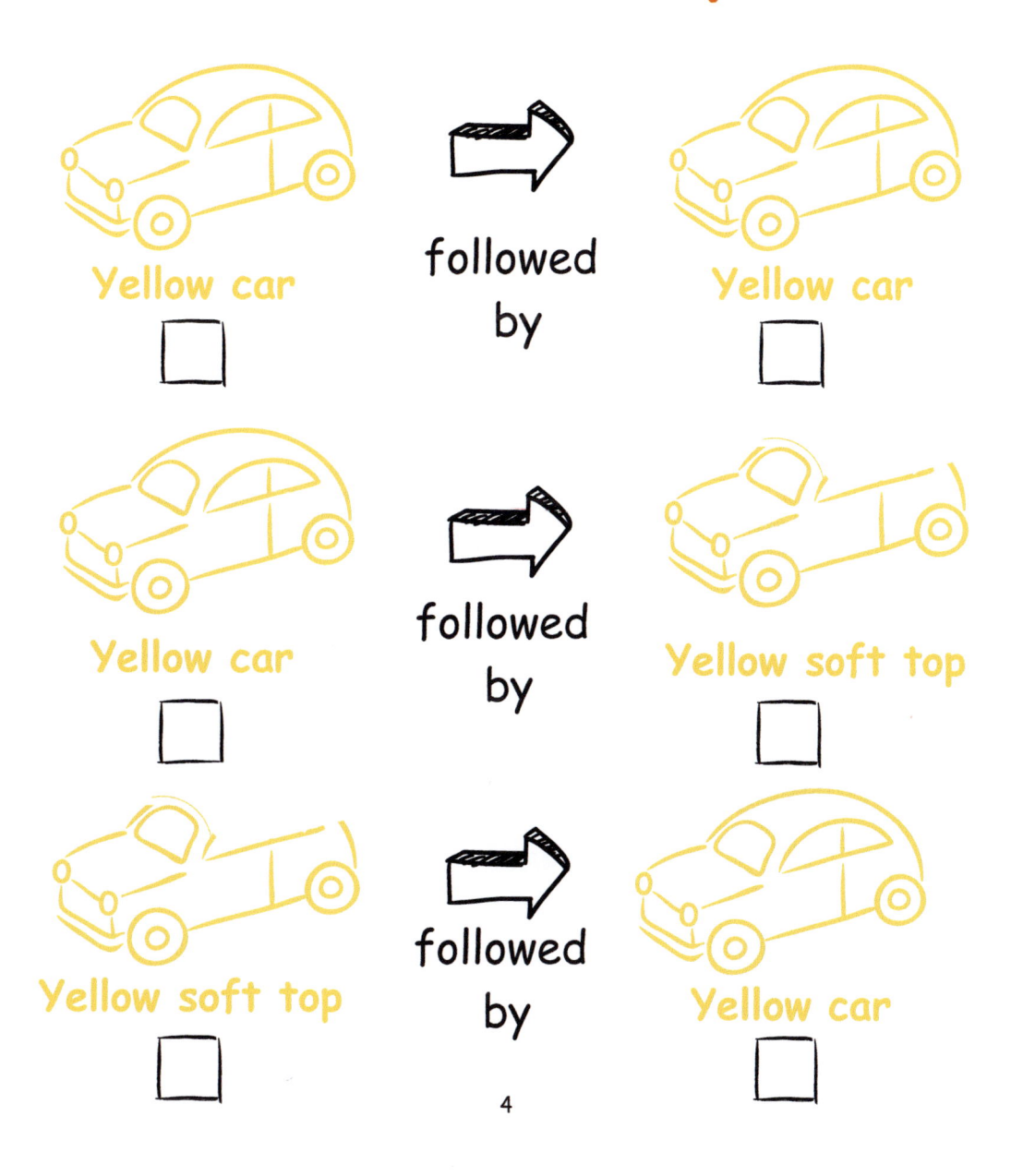

Simon Baldock

Yellow car → followed by → Yellow car ☐

Yellow car → followed by → Yellow soft top ☐

Yellow soft top → followed by → Yellow car ☐

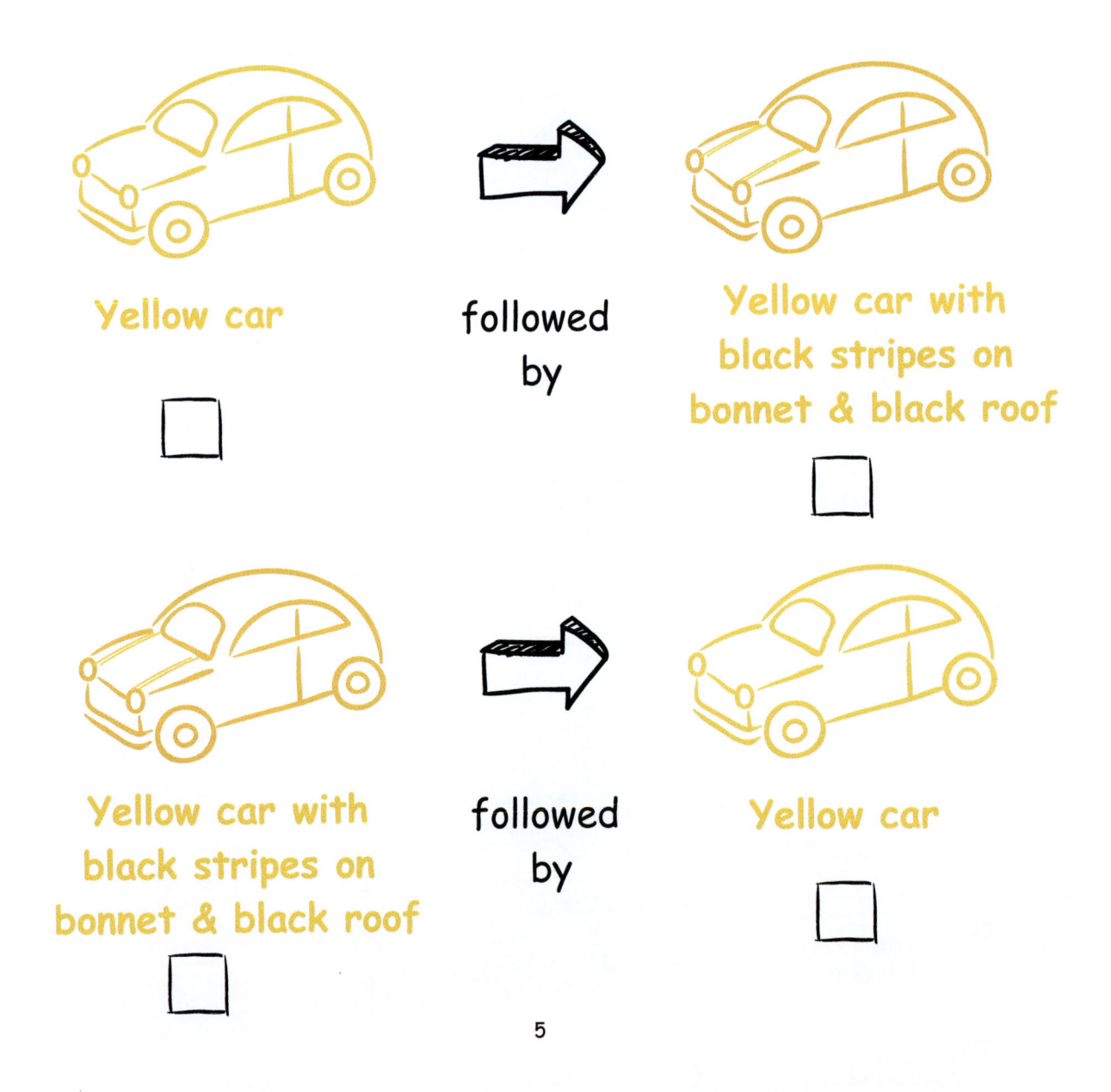

The Ultimate Yellow Car Spotters Handbook

Yellow car

☐

followed by

Yellow car with black stripes on bonnet & black roof

☐

Yellow car with black stripes on bonnet & black roof

☐

followed by

Yellow car

☐

Simon Baldock

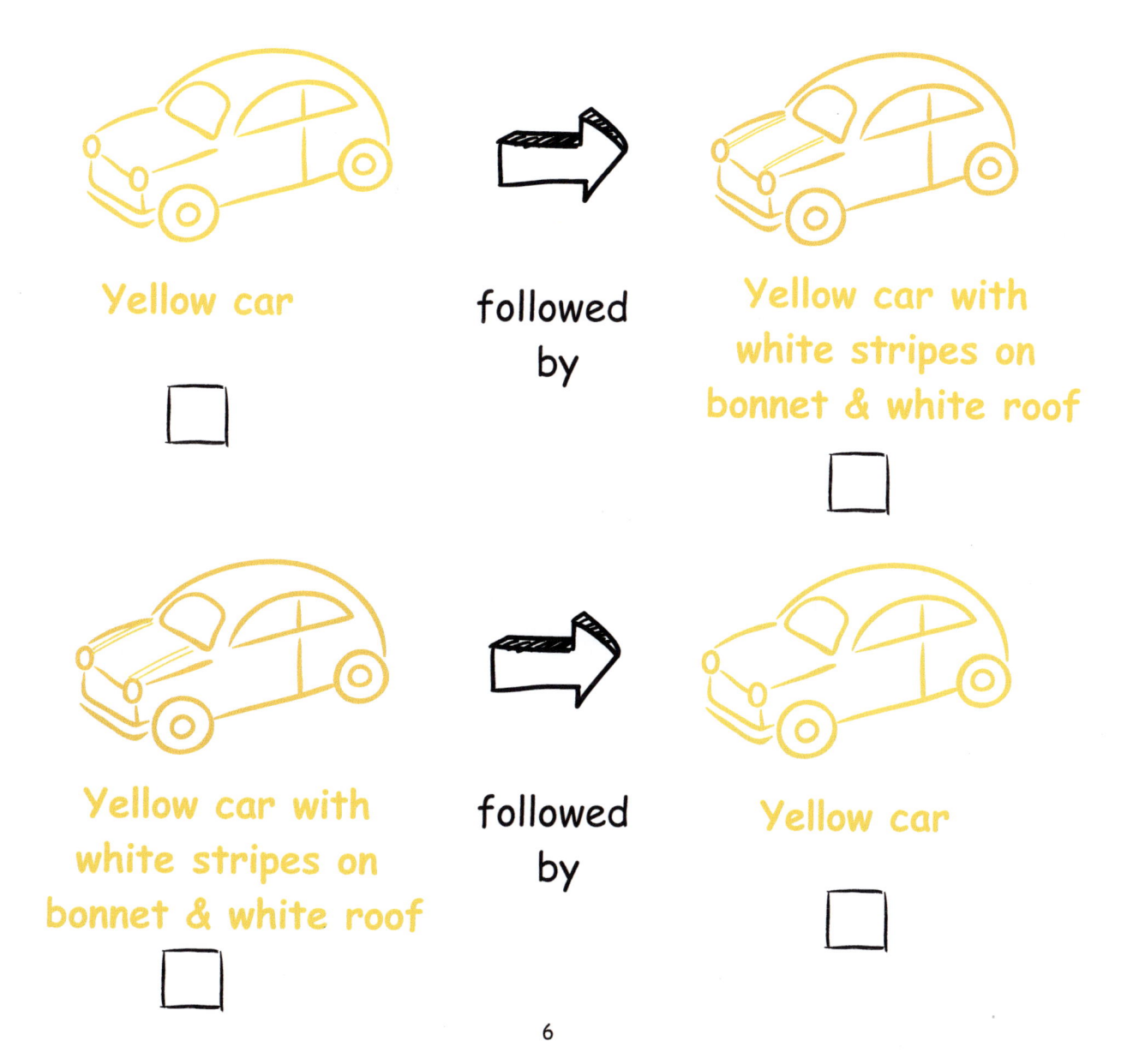

Yellow car followed by Yellow car with white stripes on bonnet & white roof

☐ ☐

Yellow car with white stripes on bonnet & white roof followed by Yellow car

☐ ☐

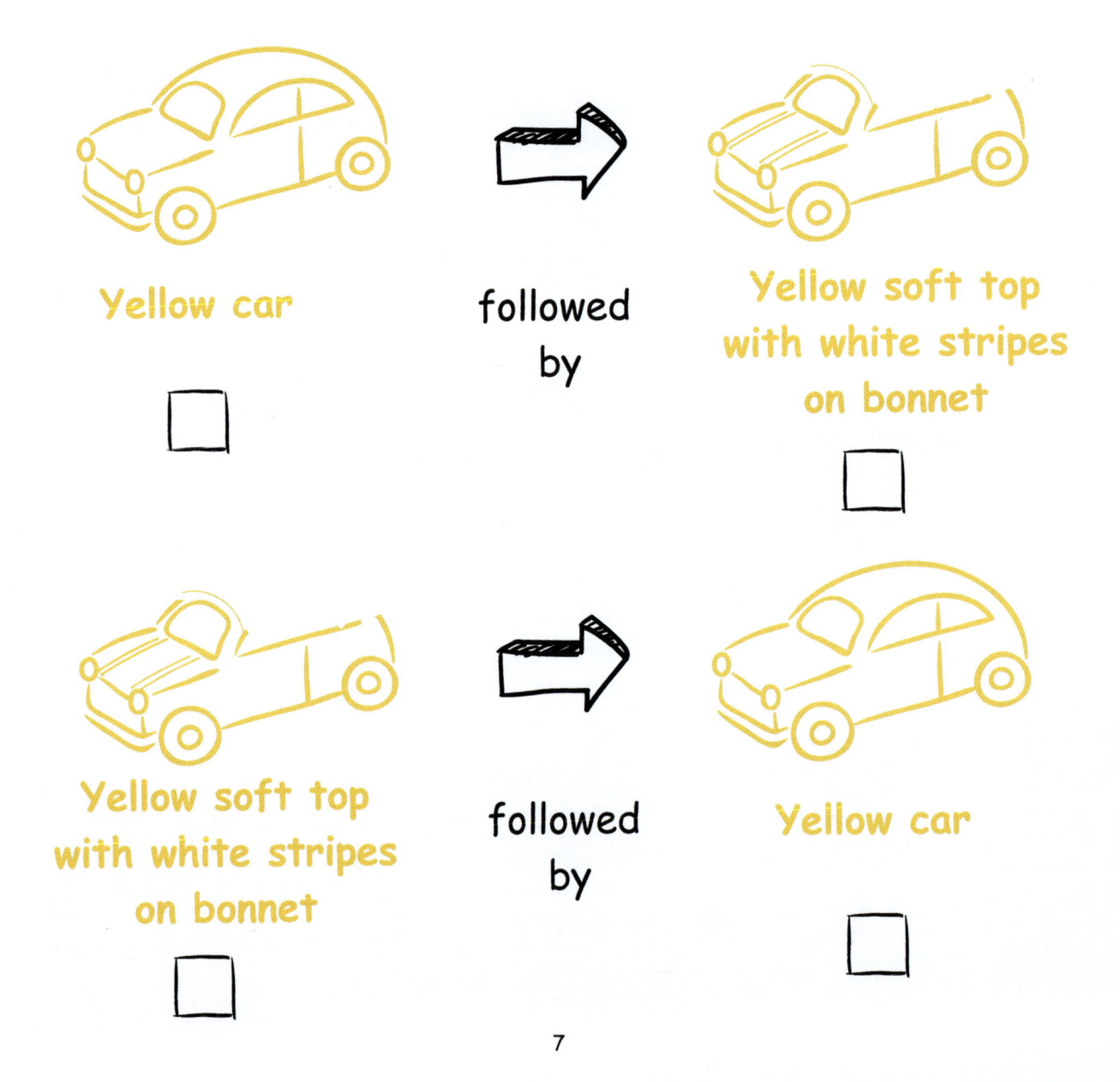

The Ultimate Yellow Car Spotters Handbook

Yellow car

☐

followed by

Yellow soft top with white stripes on bonnet

☐

Yellow soft top with white stripes on bonnet

☐

followed by

Yellow car

☐

Simon Baldock

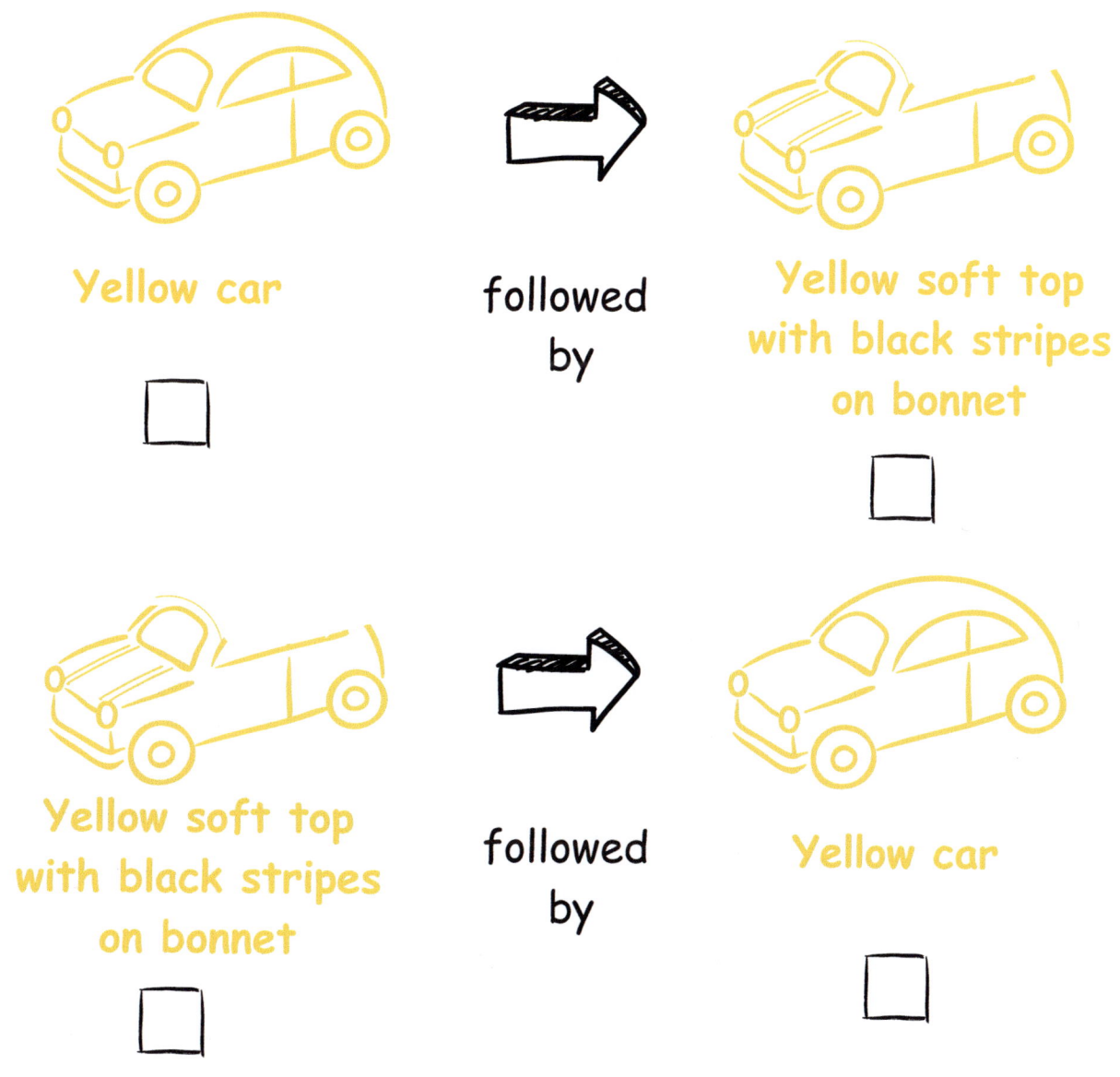

Yellow car followed by **Yellow soft top with black stripes on bonnet**

☐ ☐

Yellow soft top with black stripes on bonnet followed by **Yellow car**

☐ ☐

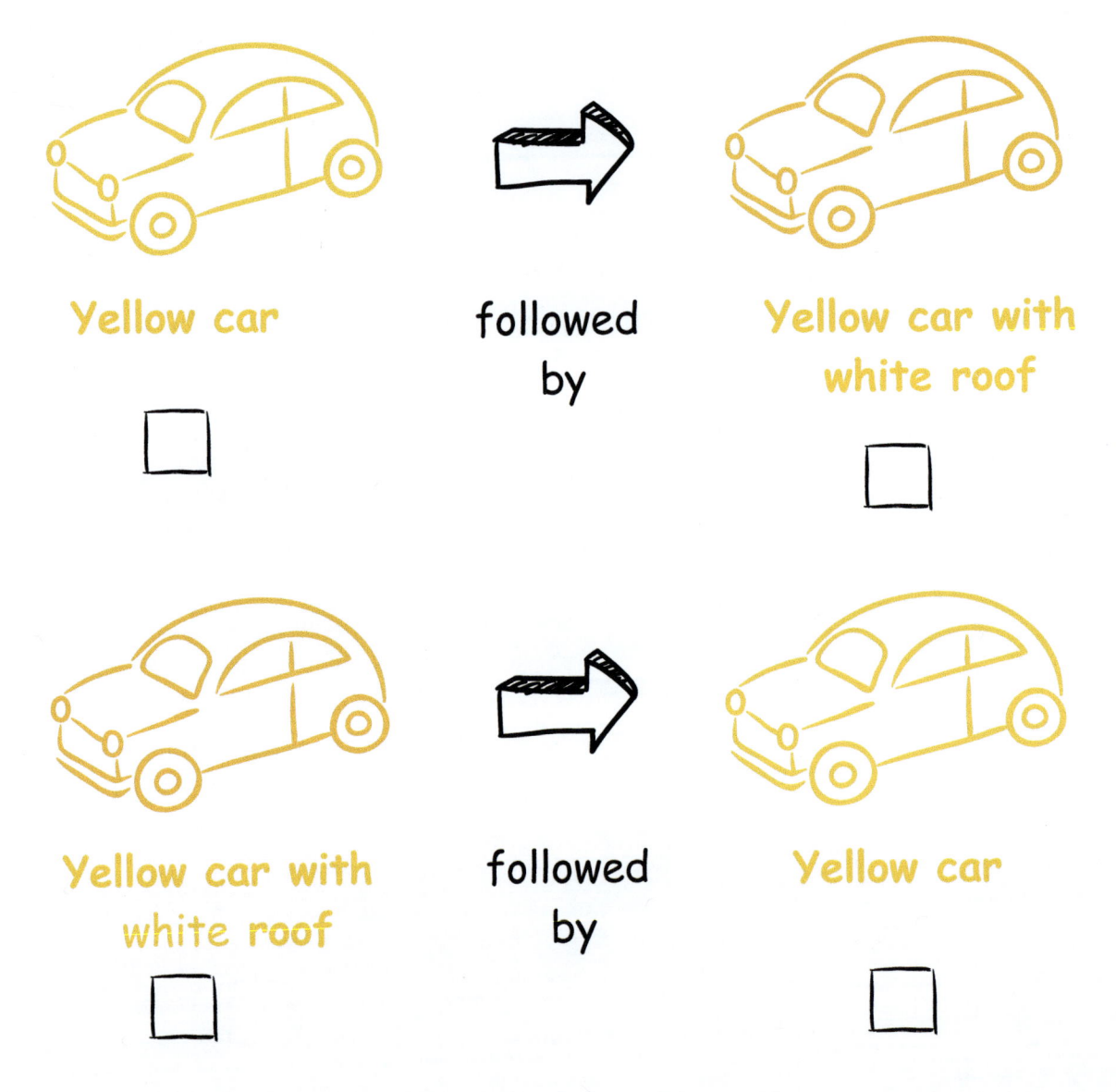

The Ultimate Yellow Car Spotters Handbook

Yellow car ☐   followed by   Yellow car with white roof ☐

Yellow car with white roof ☐   followed by   Yellow car ☐

Simon Baldock

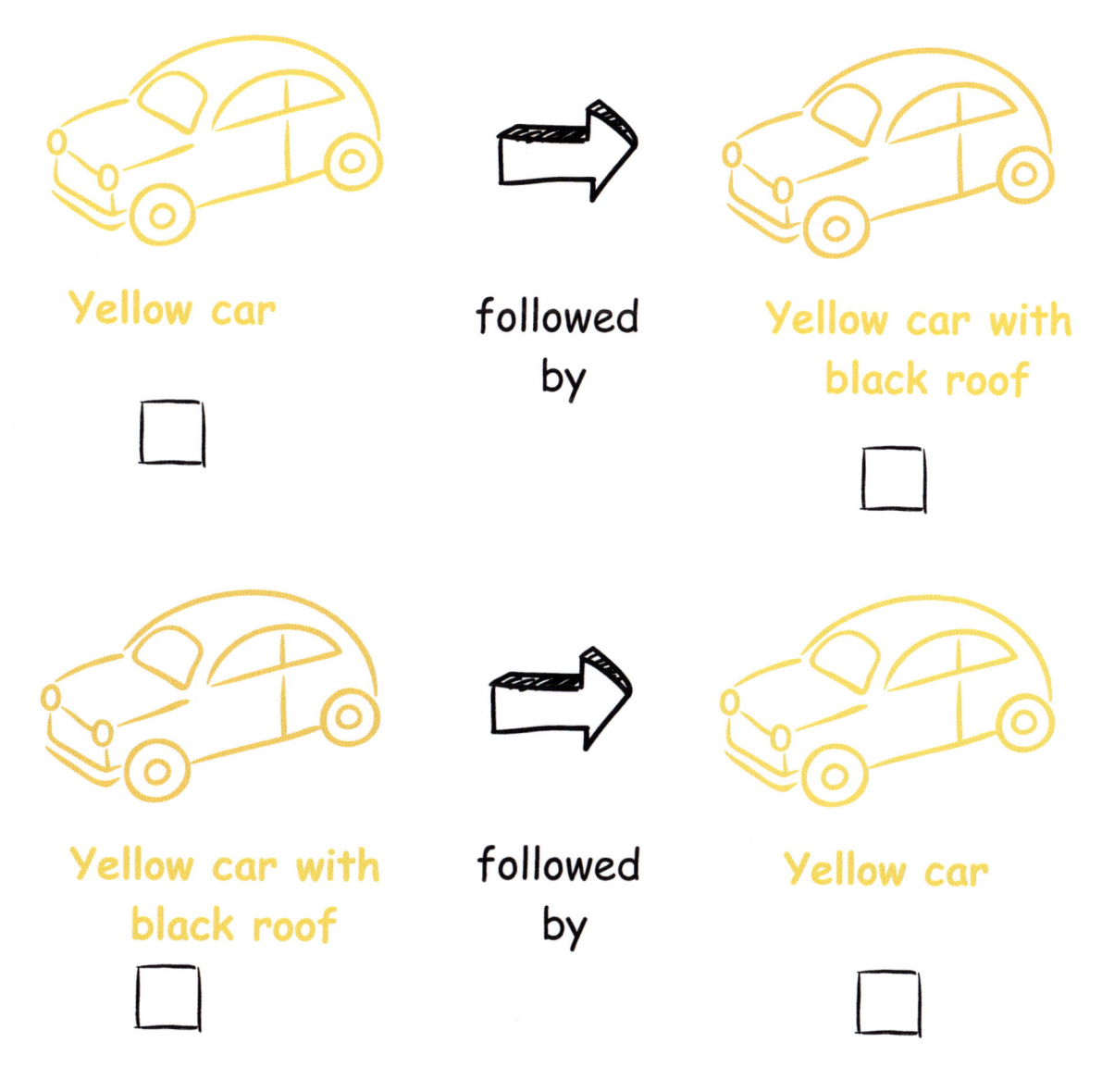

Yellow car → followed by → Yellow car with black roof

☐ ☐

Yellow car with black roof → followed by → Yellow car

☐ ☐

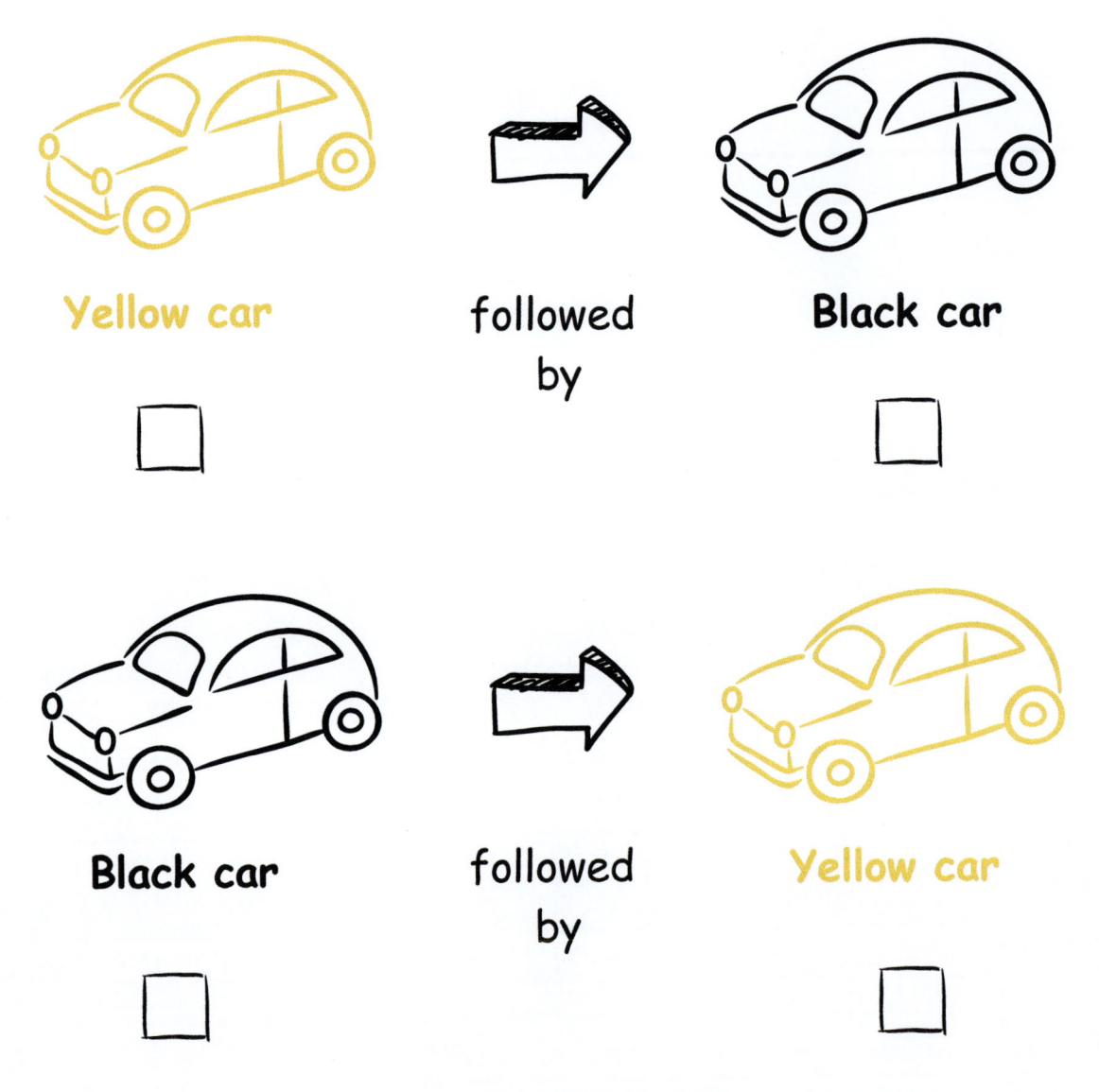

The Ultimate Yellow Car Spotters Handbook

Yellow car followed by **Black car**

☐ ☐

Black car followed by **Yellow car**

☐ ☐

Simon Baldock

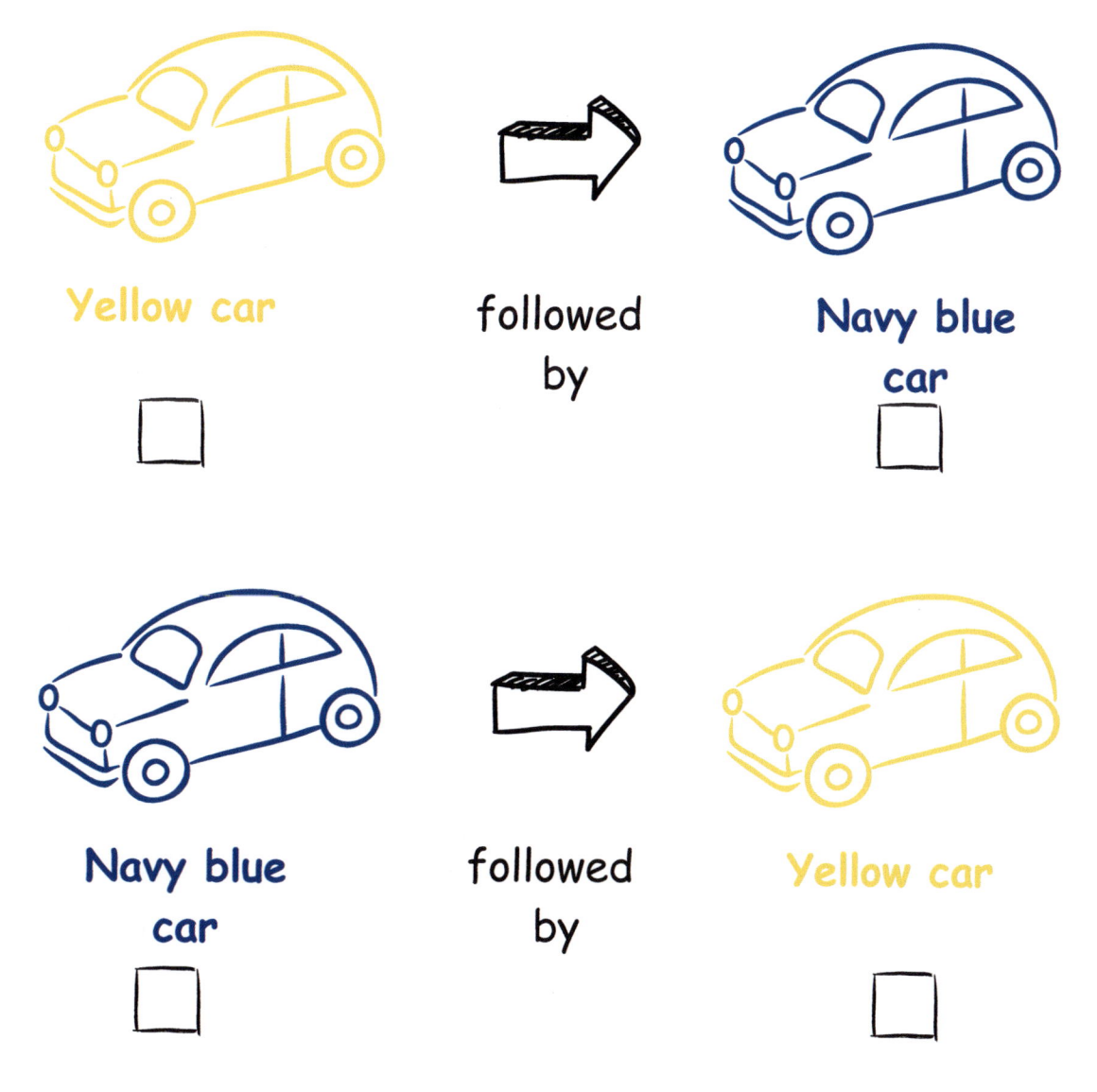

Yellow car   followed by   **Navy blue car**

☐

Navy blue car   followed by   **Yellow car**

☐

12

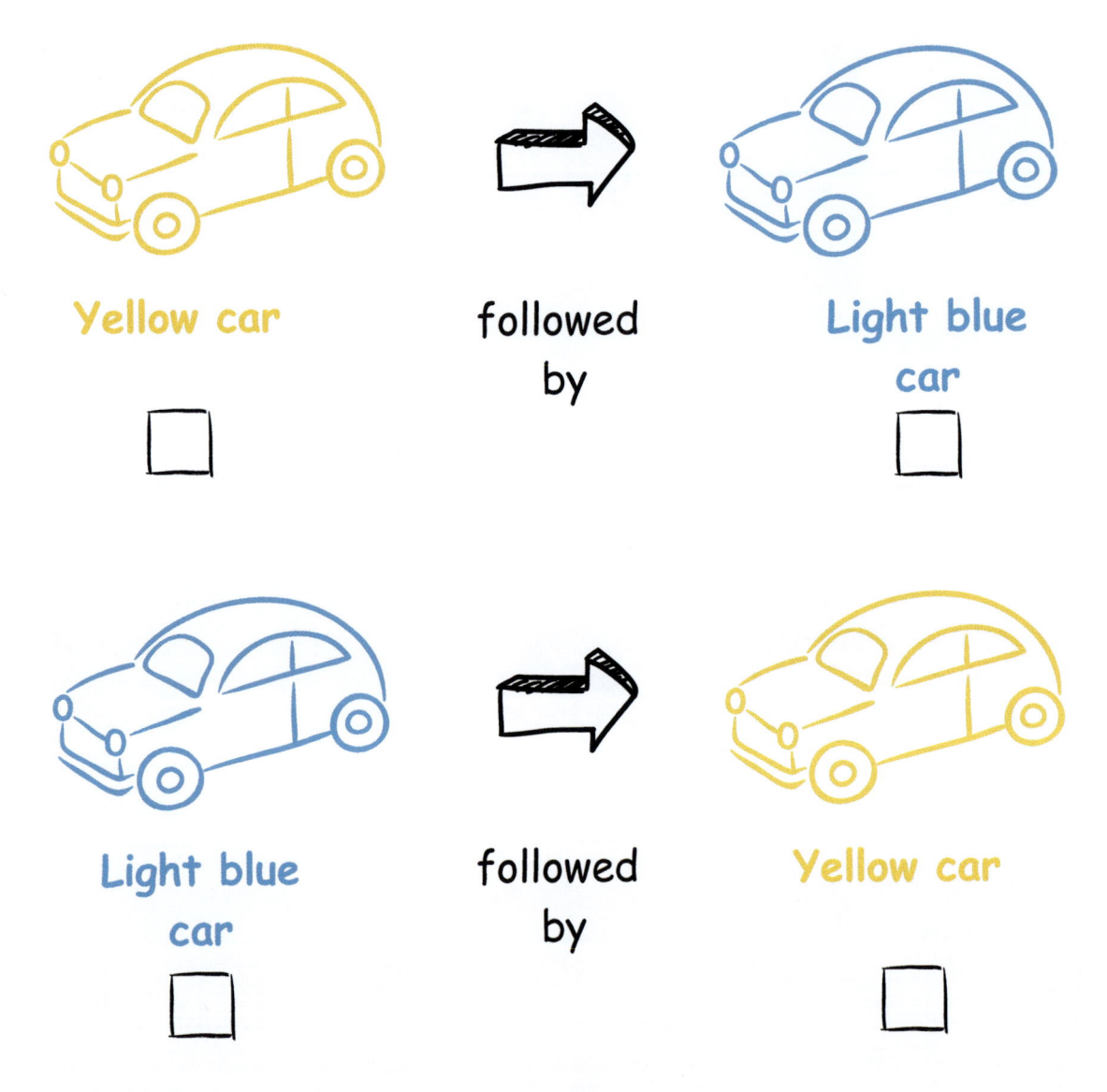

The Ultimate Yellow Car Spotters Handbook

Yellow car ☐ followed by Light blue car ☐

Light blue car ☐ followed by Yellow car ☐

Simon Baldock

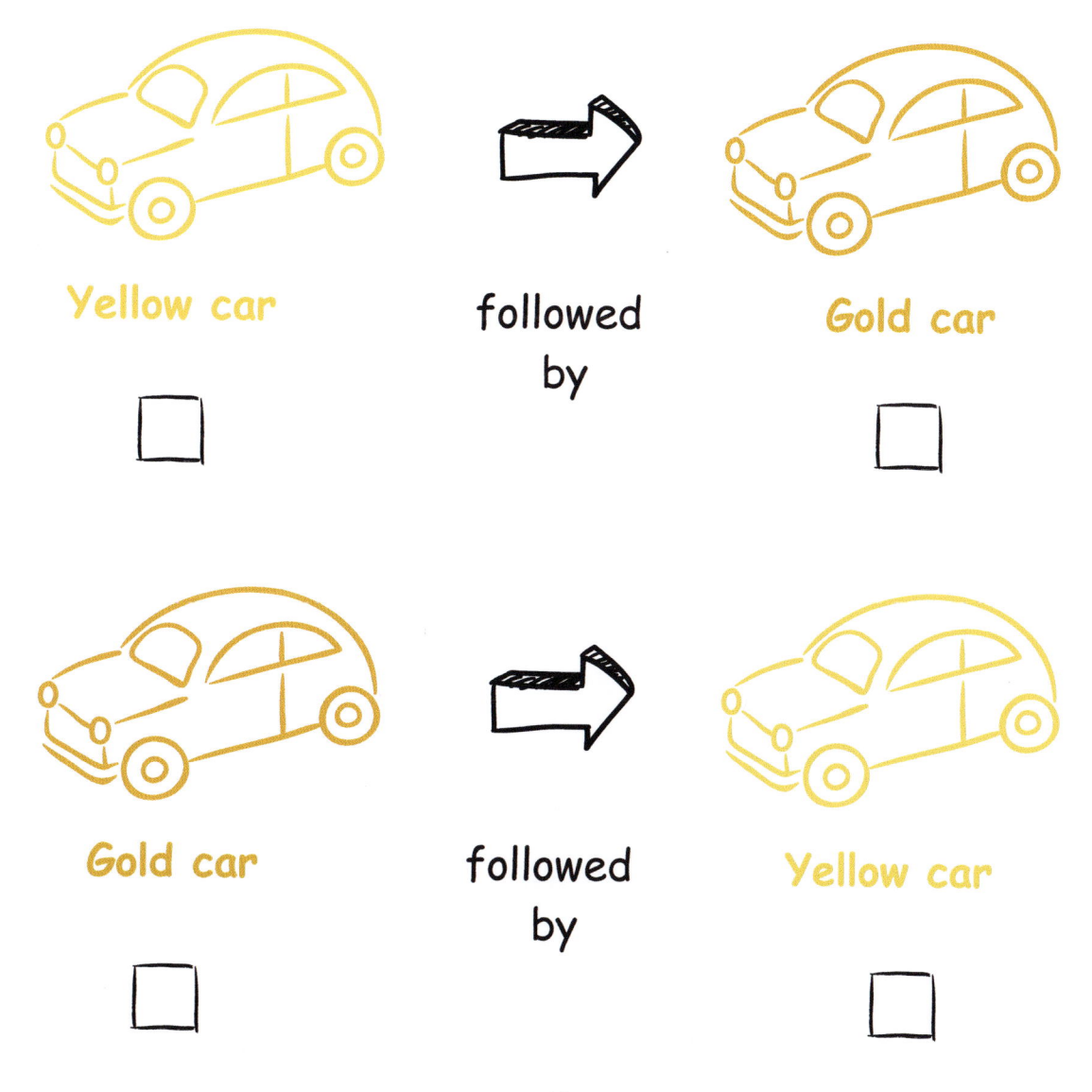

Yellow car followed by **Gold car**

☐ ☐

Gold car followed by **Yellow car**

☐ ☐

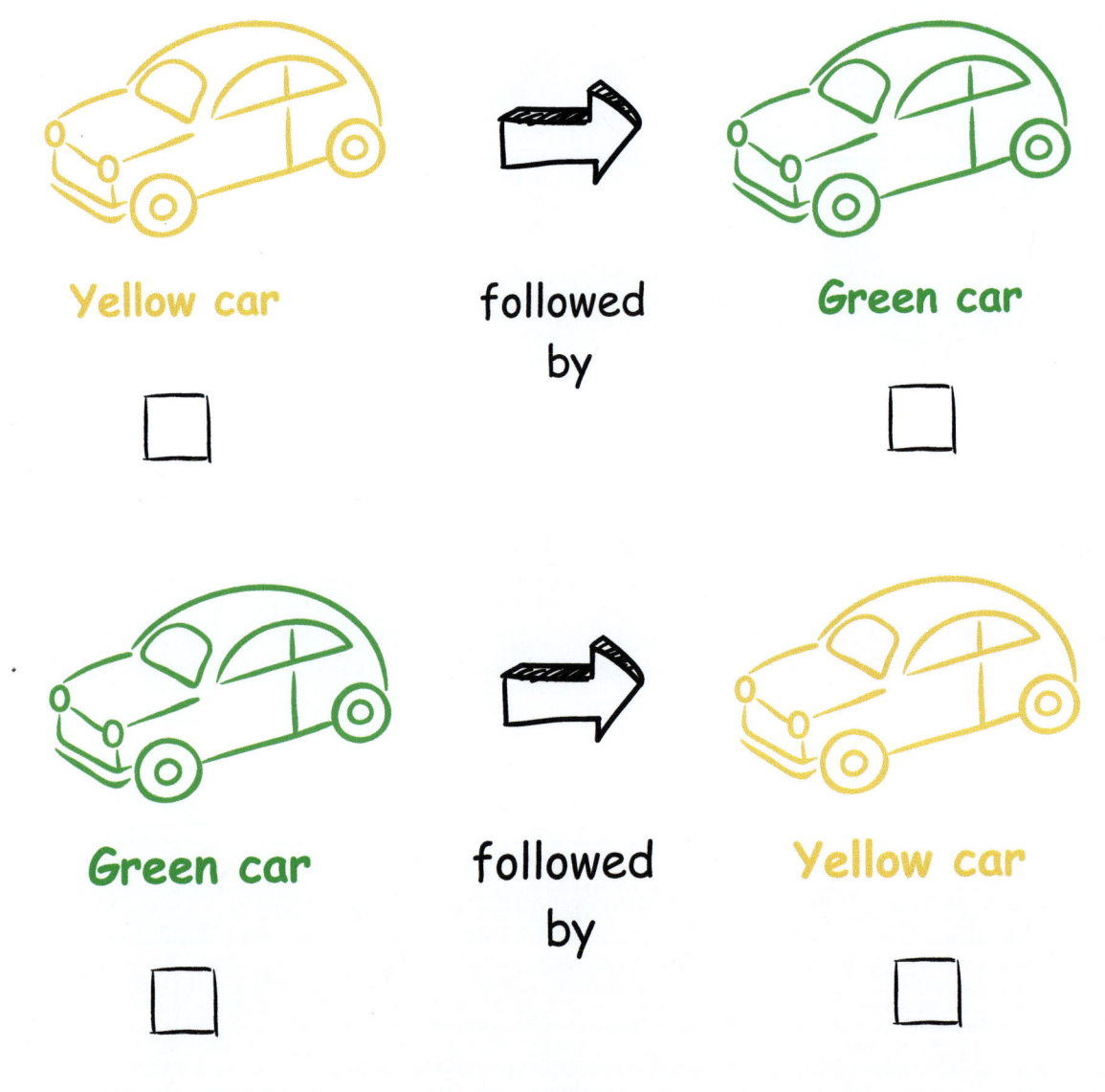

The Ultimate Yellow Car Spotters Handbook

Yellow car followed by **Green car**

☐   ☐

Green car followed by **Yellow car**

☐   ☐

Simon Baldock

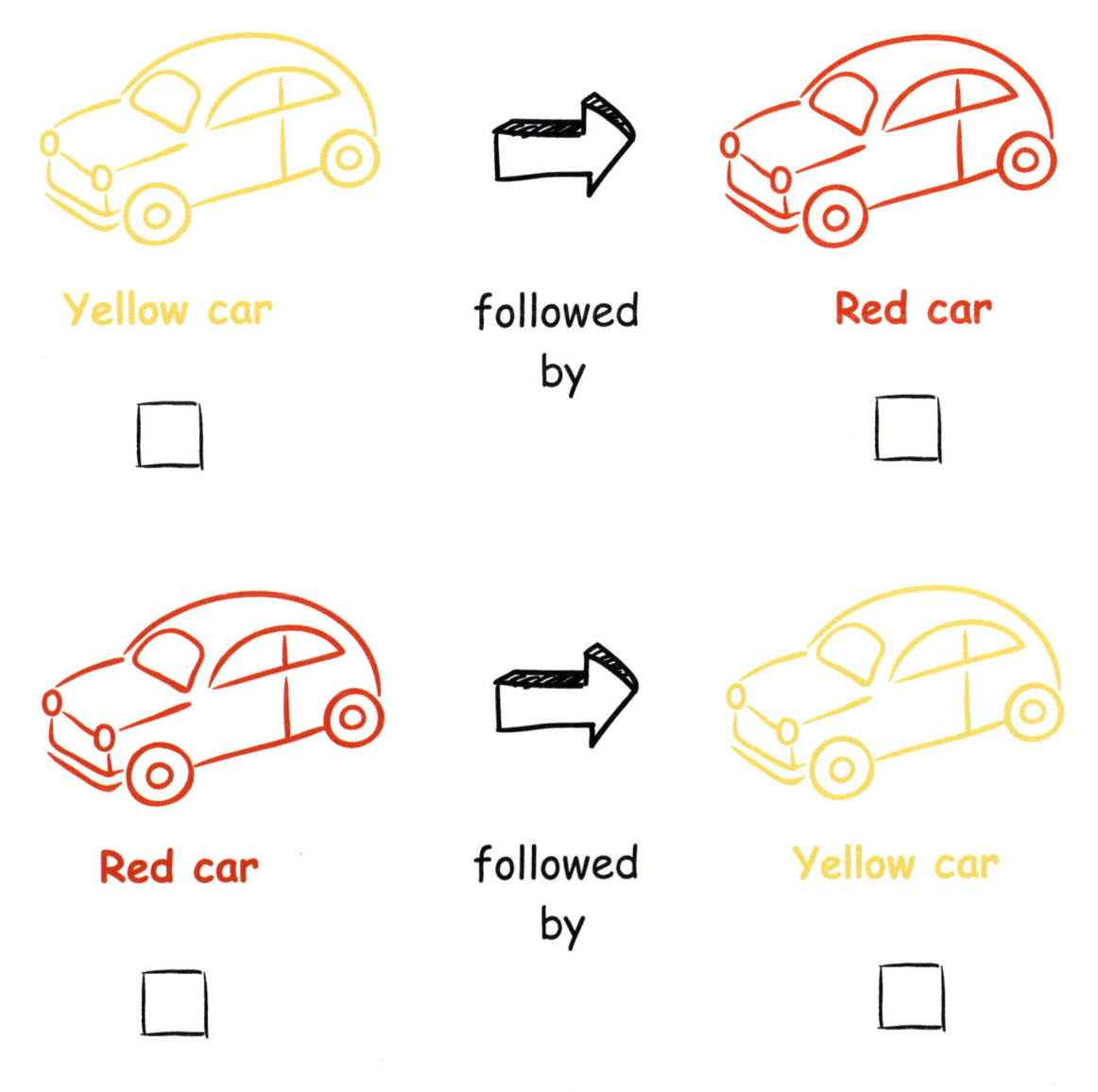

Yellow car   followed by   Red car

☐   ☐

Red car   followed by   Yellow car

☐   ☐

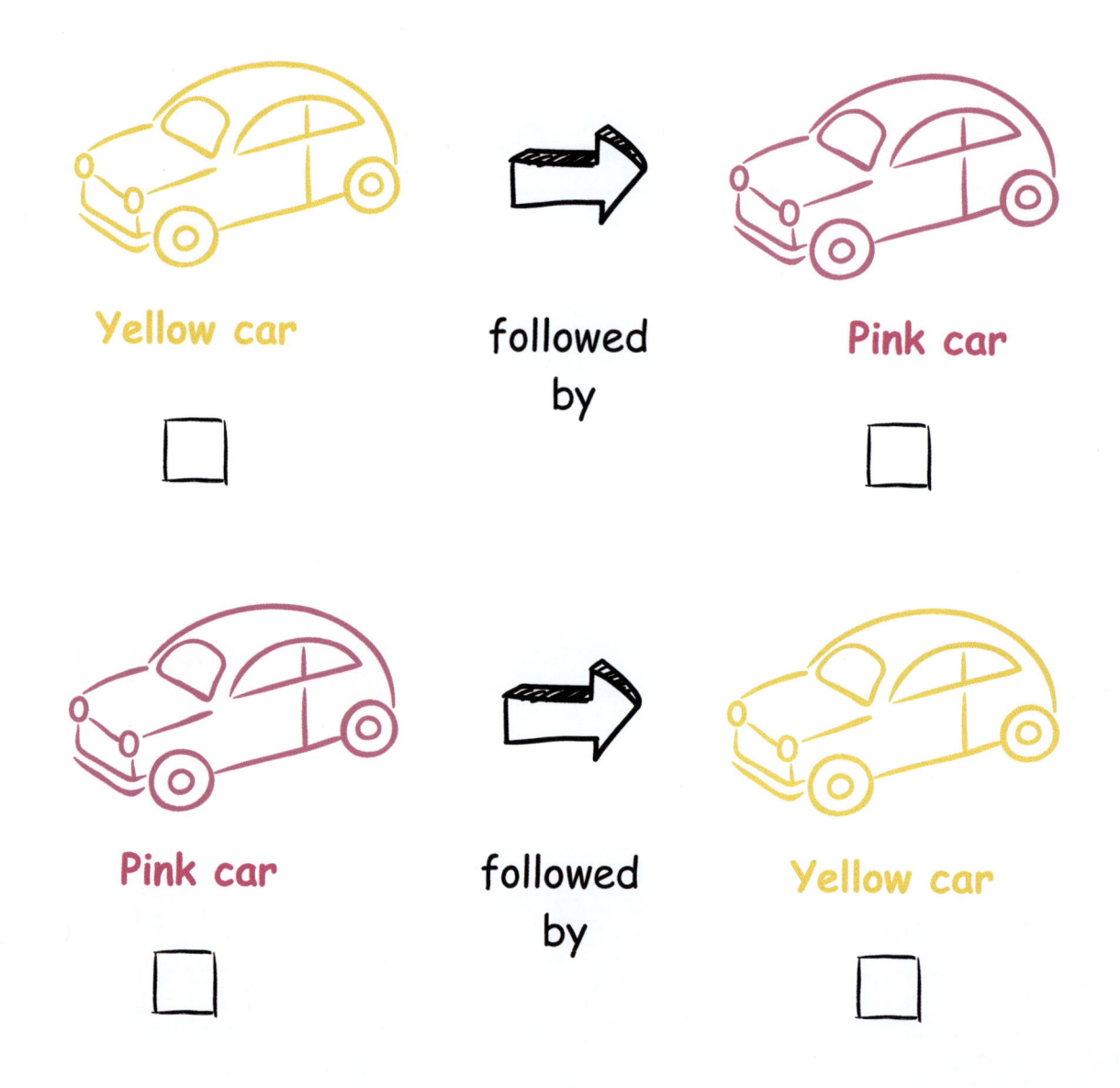

The Ultimate Yellow Car Spotters Handbook

Yellow car ➡ followed by ➡ Pink car
☐ ☐

Pink car ➡ followed by ➡ Yellow car
☐ ☐

Simon Baldock

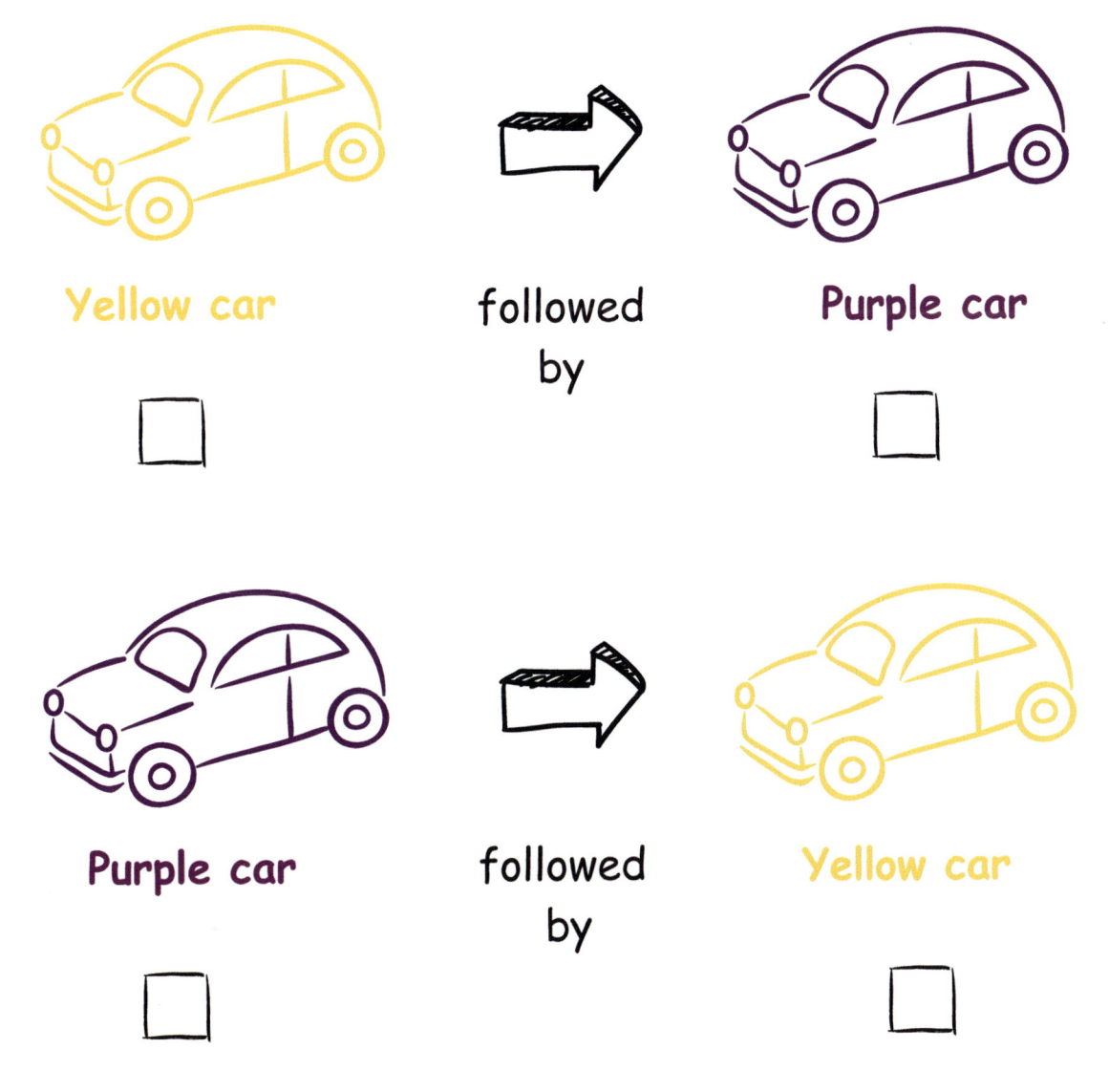

Yellow car   followed by   Purple car

☐   ☐

Purple car   followed by   Yellow car

☐   ☐

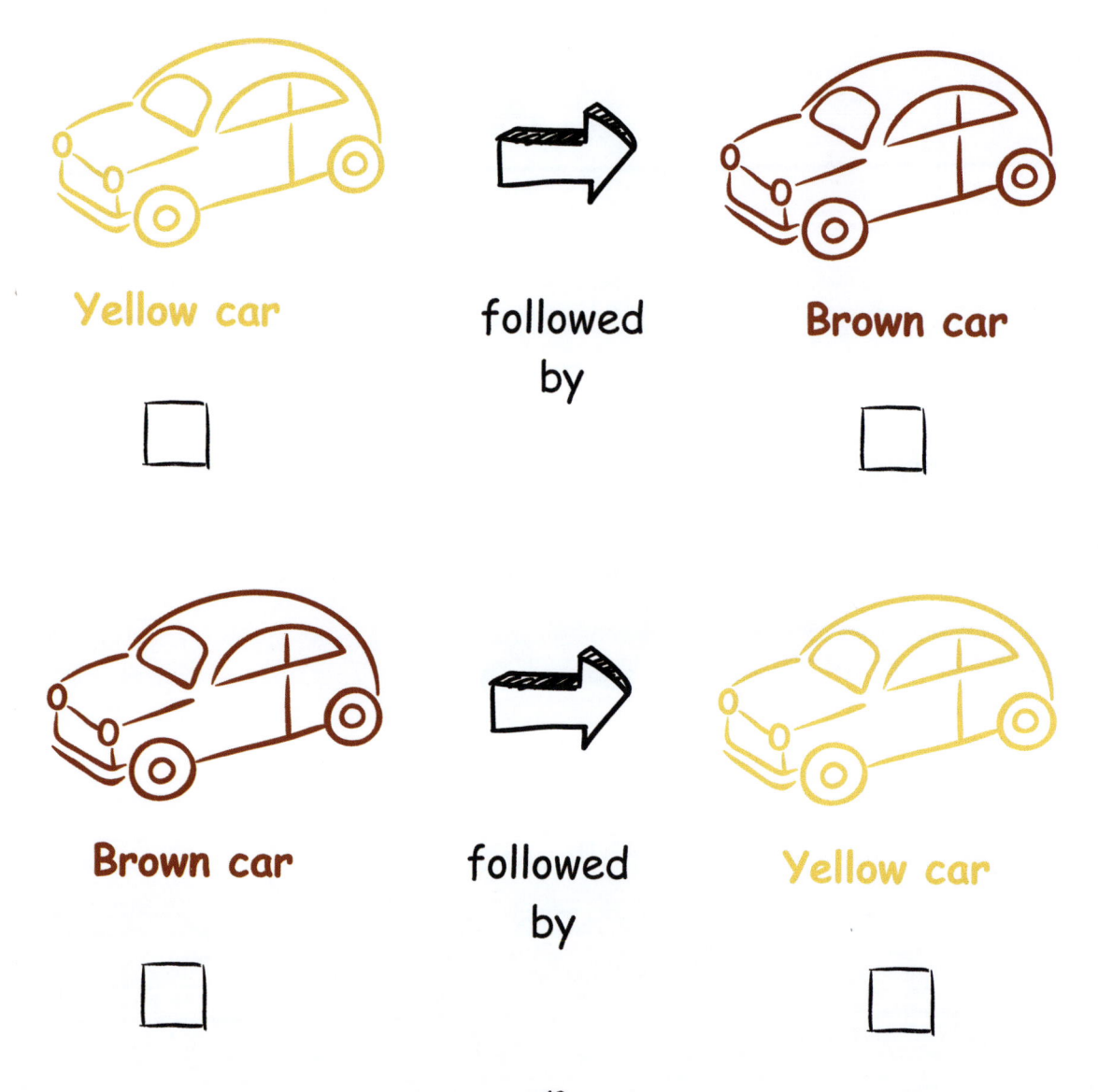

The Ultimate Yellow Car Spotters Handbook

Yellow car followed by **Brown car**

Brown car followed by **Yellow car**

Simon Baldock

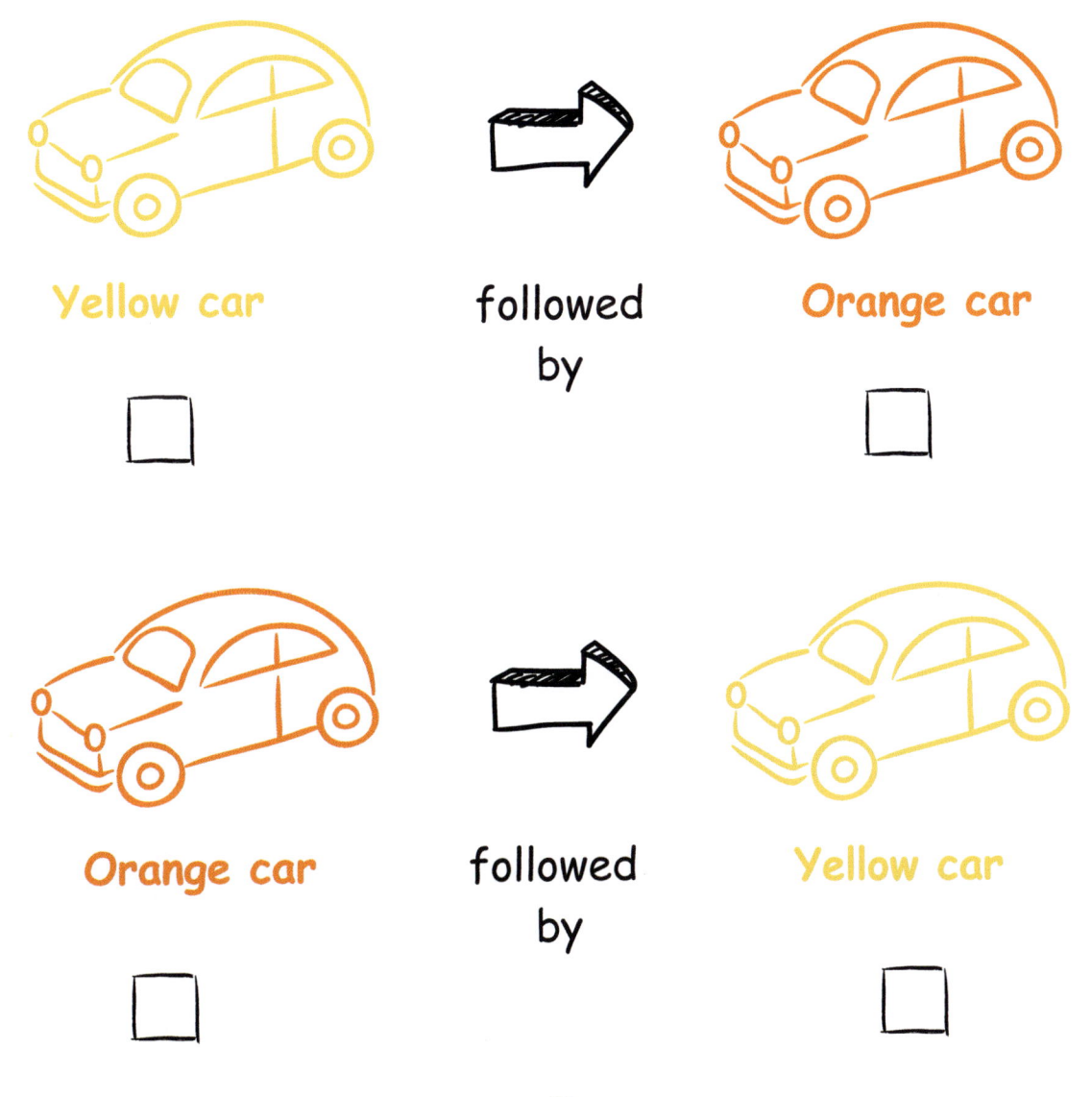

Yellow car followed by **Orange car**

☐ ☐

Orange car followed by **Yellow car**

☐ ☐

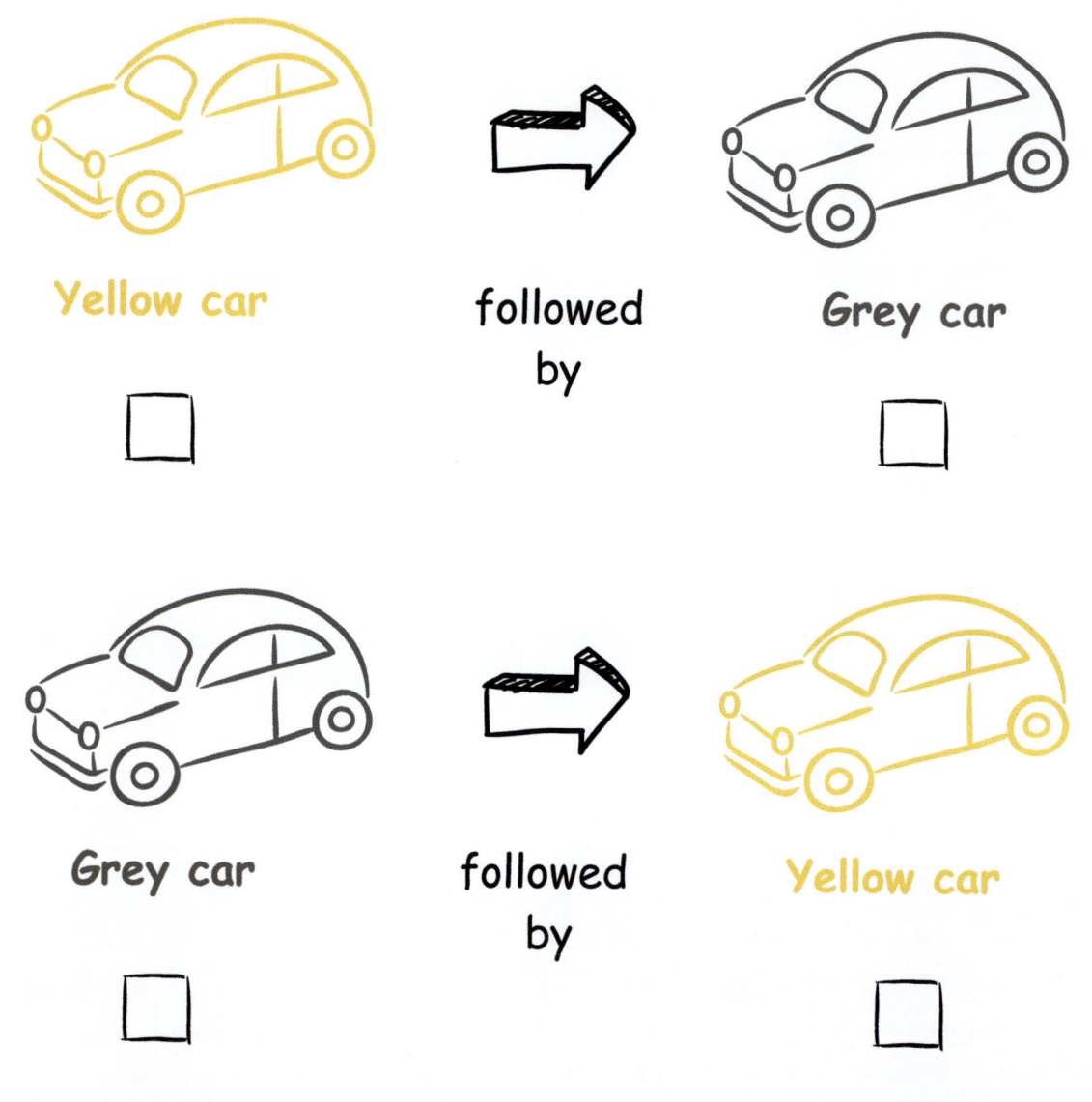

The Ultimate Yellow Car Spotters Handbook

Yellow car followed by Grey car

☐   ☐

Grey car followed by Yellow car

☐   ☐

21

Simon Baldock

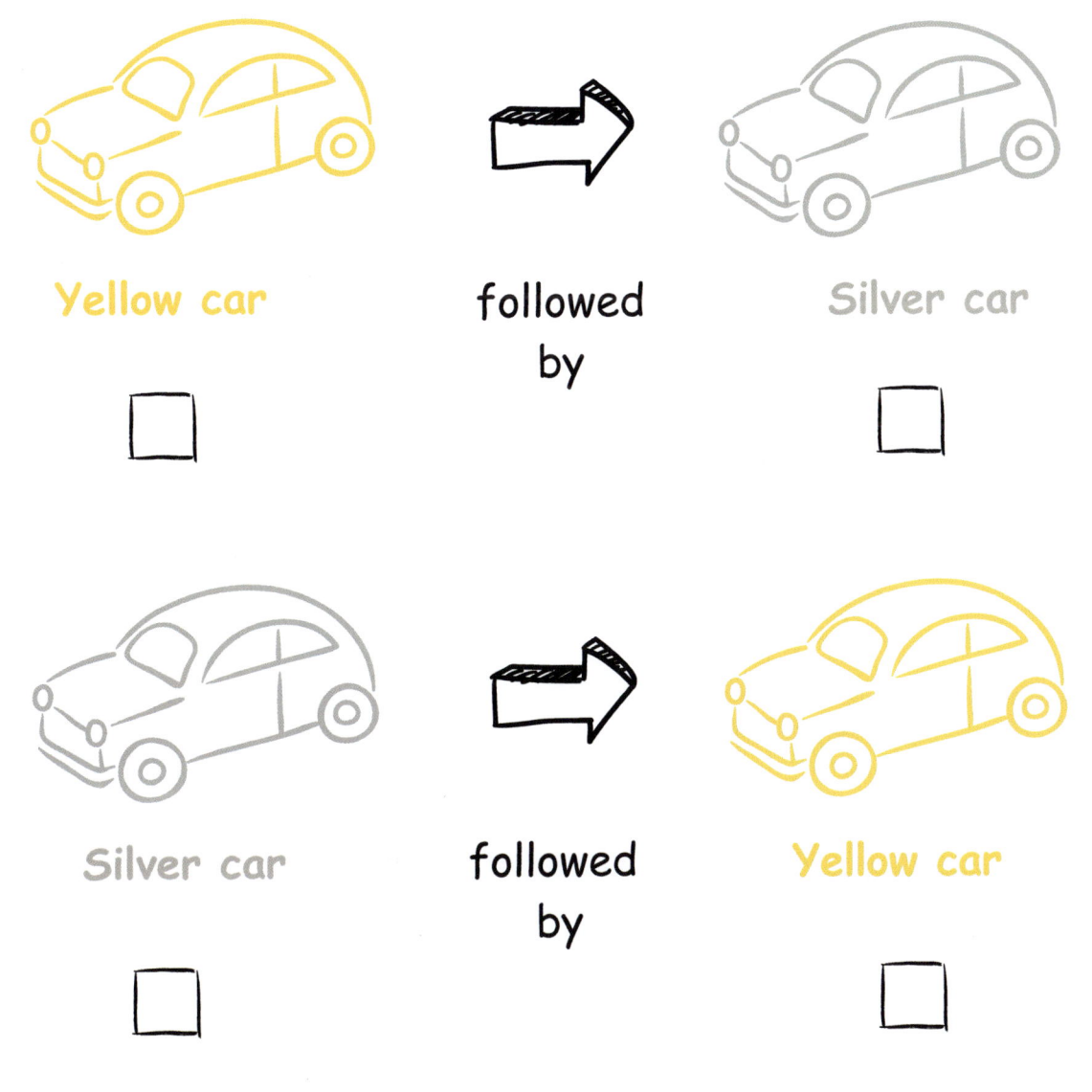

Yellow car   followed by   Silver car

☐   ☐

Silver car   followed by   **Yellow car**

☐   ☐

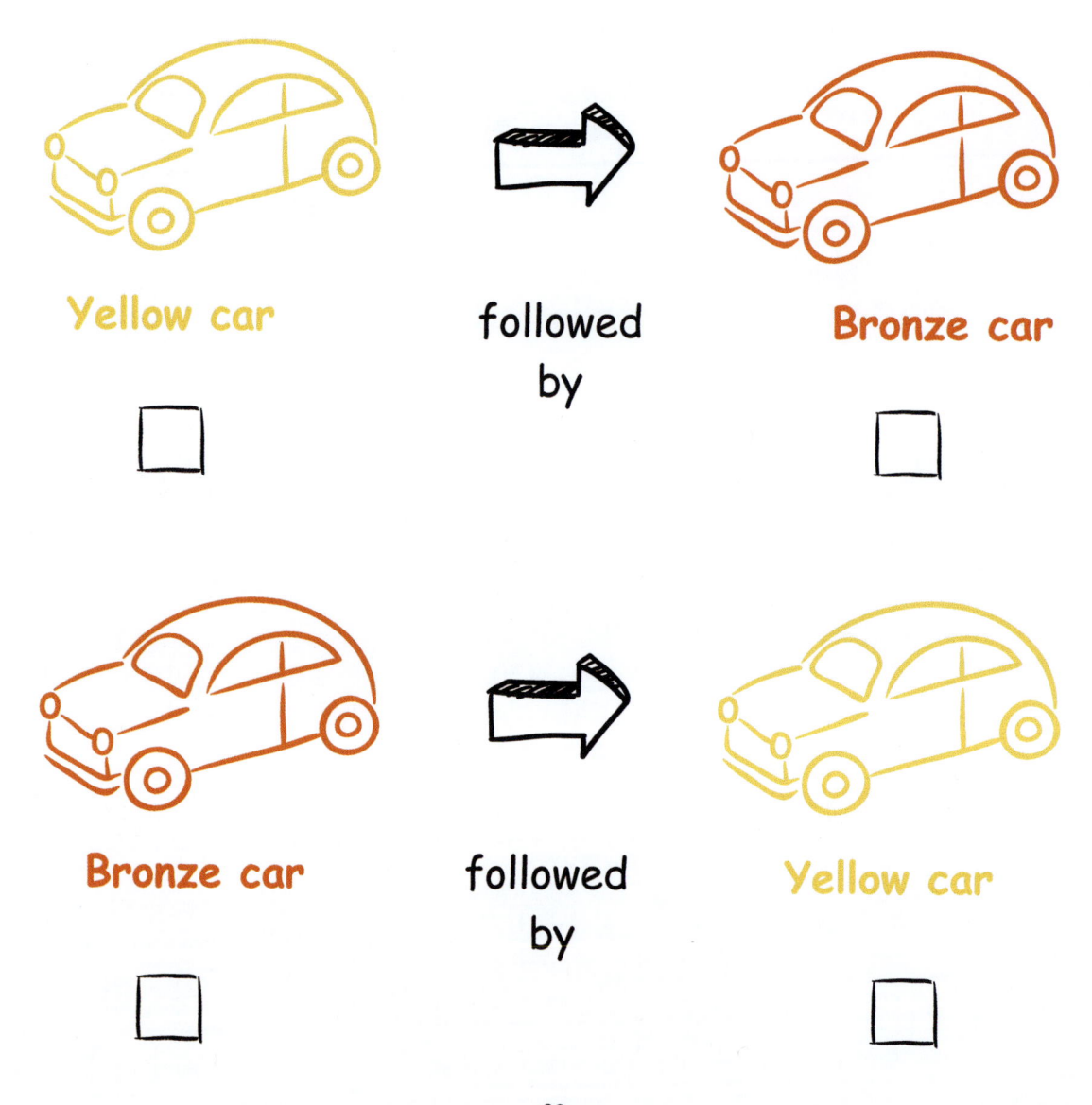

The Ultimate Yellow Car Spotters Handbook

Yellow car   followed by   Bronze car

□   □

Bronze car   followed by   Yellow car

□   □

23

Simon Baldock

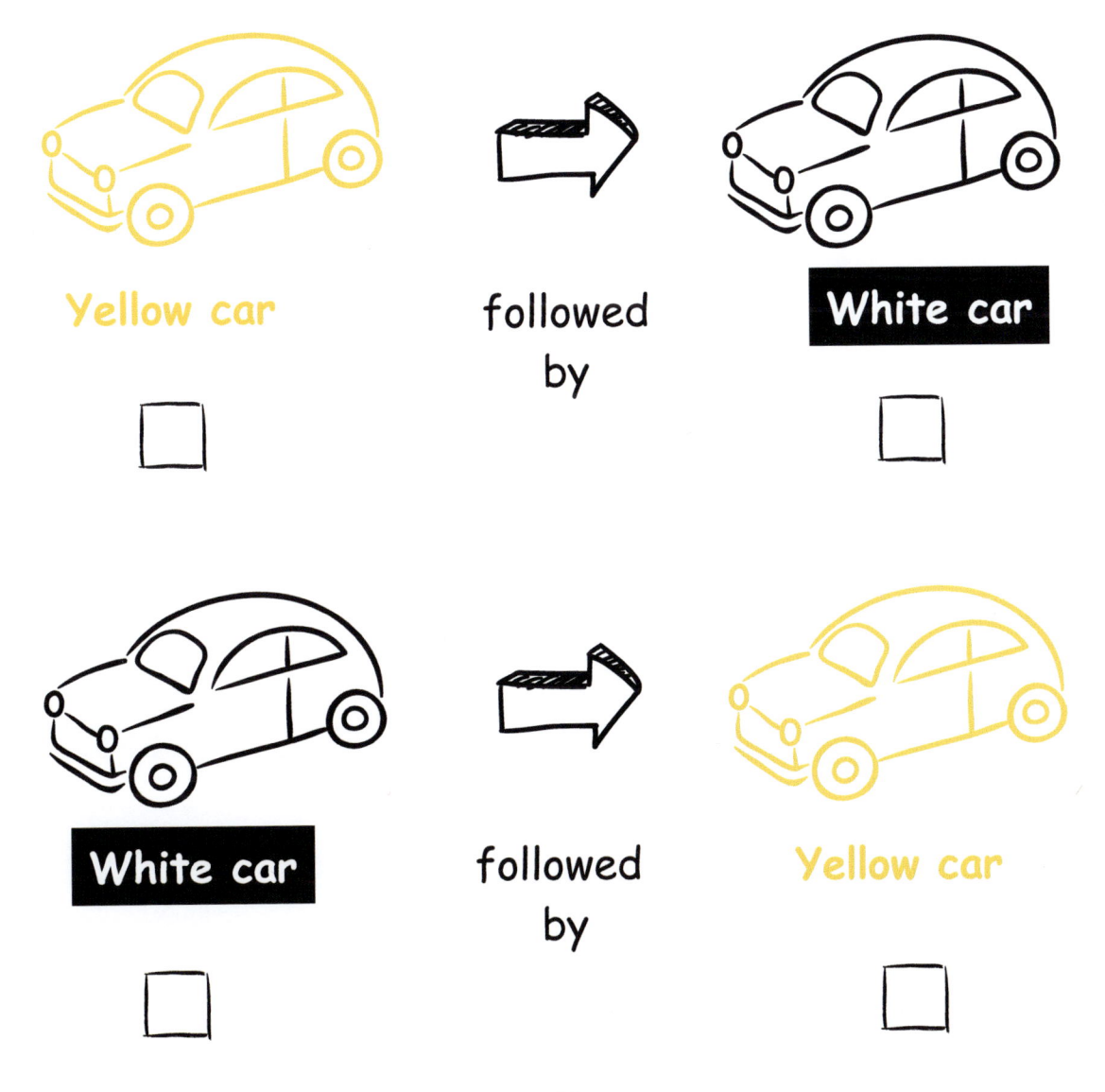

Yellow car followed by **White car**

☐ ☐

White car followed by Yellow car

☐ ☐

24

The Ultimate Yellow Car Spotters Handbook

Bonus pages

Yellow car towing caravan

☐

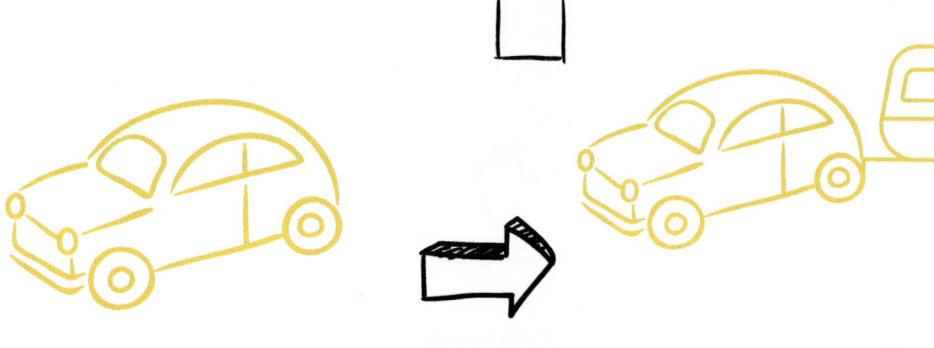

Yellow car

☐

followed by

Yellow car towing caravan

☐

Simon Baldock

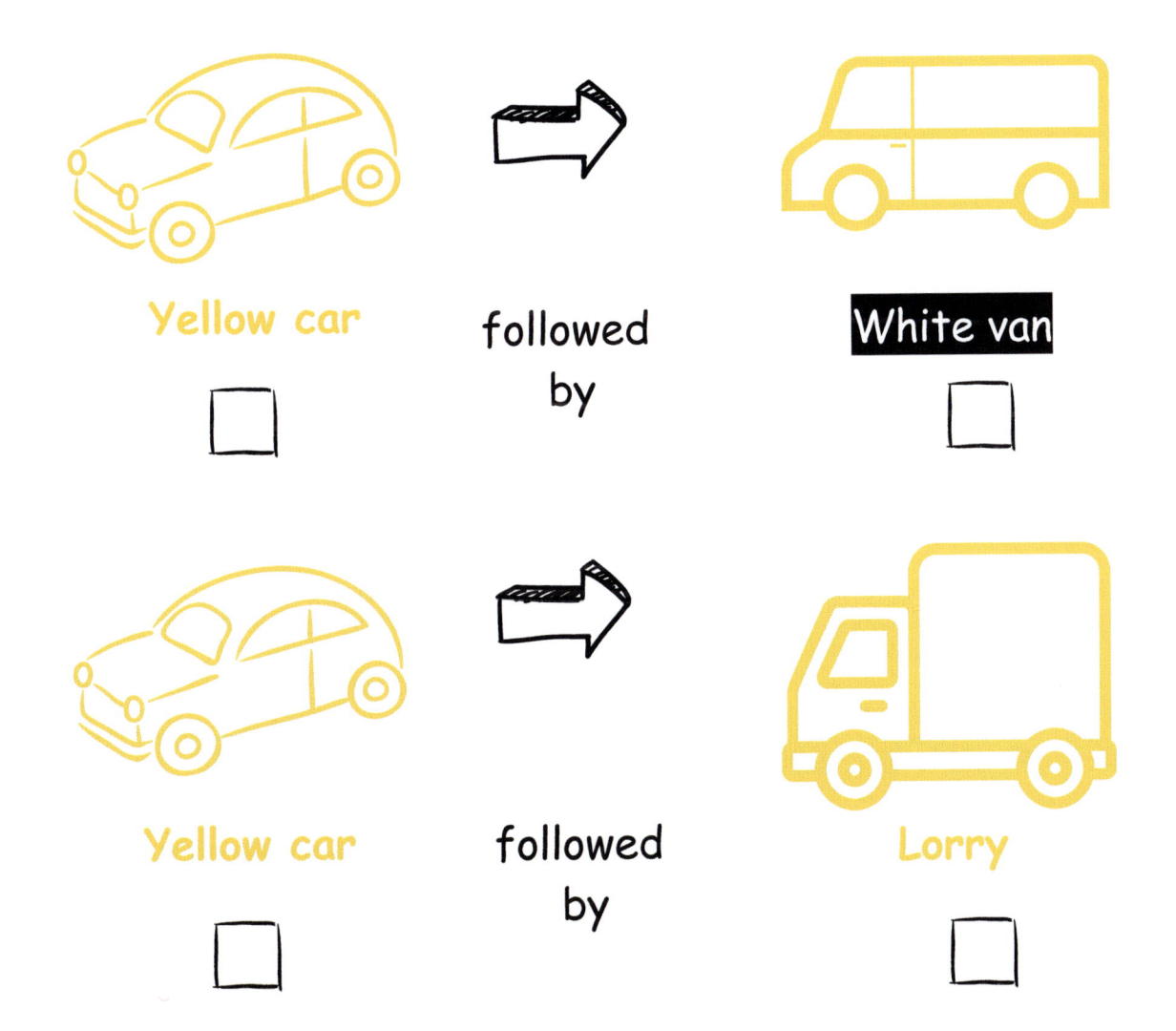

Yellow car followed by White van

☐ ☐

Yellow car followed by Lorry

☐ ☐

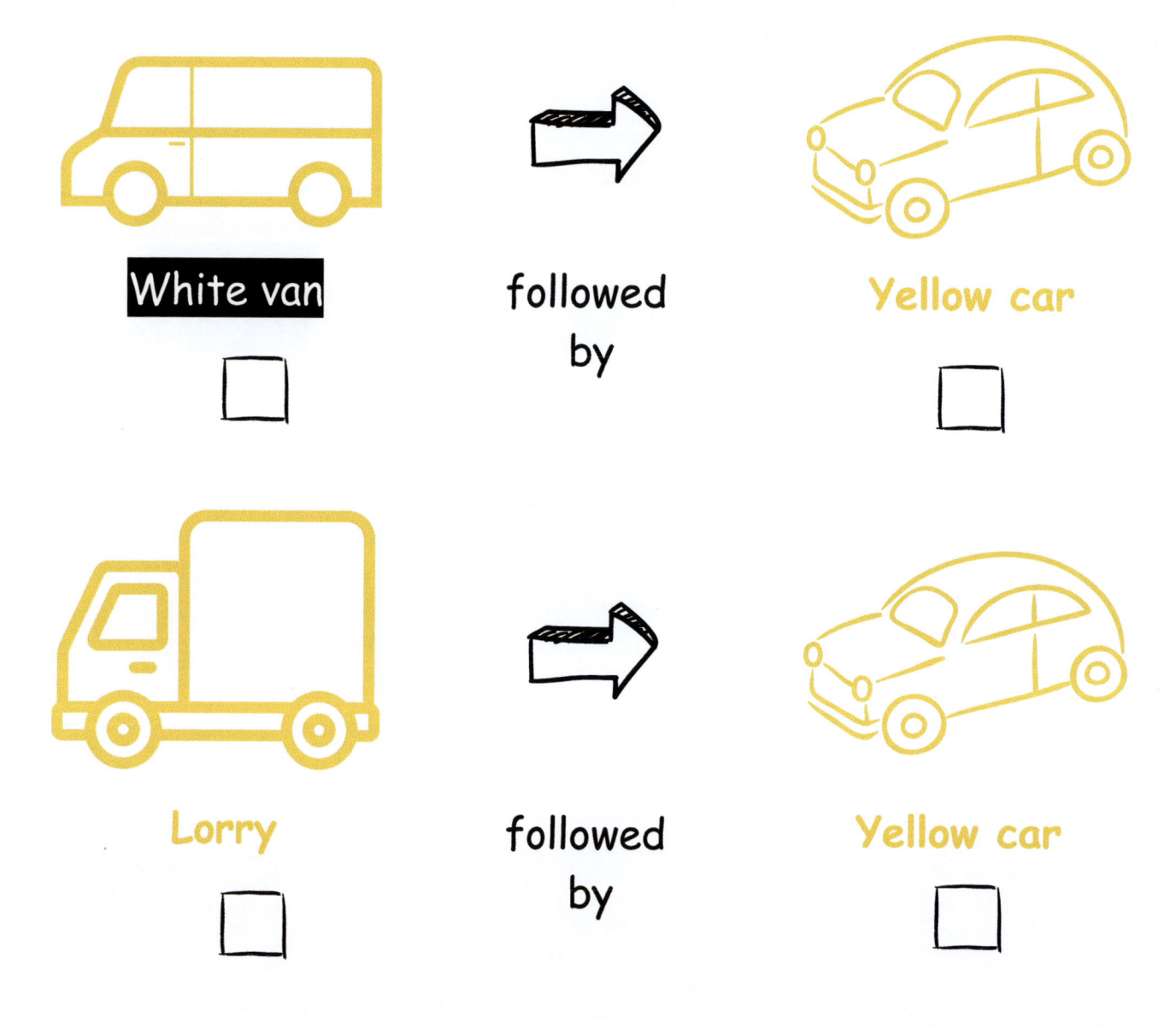

The Ultimate Yellow Car Spotters Handbook

White van followed by Yellow car
☐   ☐

Lorry followed by Yellow car
☐   ☐

NOTES:

Printed in Great Britain
by Amazon